📖 DORLING KINDERSLEY *READERS*

Level 1
Beginning to Read

A Day at Greenhill Farm
Truck Trouble
Tale of a Tadpole
Surprise Puppy!
Duckling Days
A Day at Seagull Beach
Whatever the Weather
Busy Buzzy Bee
Big Machines
Wild Baby Animals
LEGO: Trouble at the Bridge
A Bed for the Winter
Born to be a Butterfly

Level 2
Beginning to Read Alone

Dinosaur Dinners
Fire Fighter!
Bugs! Bugs! Bugs!
Slinky, Scaly Snakes!
Animal Hospital
The Little Ballerina
Munching, Crunching, Sniffing,
 and Snooping
The Secret Life of Trees
Winking, Blinking, Wiggling,
 and Waggling
Astronaut – Living in Space
LEGO: Castle Under Attack!
Twisters!
Holiday! Celebration Days around
 the World

Level 3
Reading Alone

Spacebusters
Beastly Tales
Shark Attack!
Titanic
Invaders from Outer Space
Movie Magic
Plants Bite Back!
Time Traveler
Bermuda Triangle
Tiger Tales
Aladdin
Heidi
LEGO: Mission to the Arctic
Zeppelin – The Age of
 the Airship
Spies

Level 4
Proficient Readers

Days of the Knights
Volcanoes
Secrets of the Mummies
Pirates!
Horse Heroes
Trojan Horse
Micromonsters
Going for Gold!
Extreme Machines
Flying Ace – The Story of
 Amelia Earhart
Robin Hood
Black Beauty
LEGO: Race for Survival
Free at Last! The Story of
 Martin Luther King, Jr.
Joan of Arc
Spooky Spinechillers

A Note to Parents

Dorling Kindersley Readers is a compelling new program for beginning readers, designed in conjunction with leading literacy experts, including Dr. Linda Gambrell, President of the National Reading Conference and past board member of the International Reading Association.

Beautiful illustrations and superb full-color photographs combine with engaging, easy-to-read stories to offer a fresh approach to each subject in the series. Each *Dorling Kindersley Reader* is guaranteed to capture a child's interest while developing his or her reading skills, general knowledge, and love of reading.

The four levels of *Dorling Kindersley Readers* are aimed at different reading abilities, enabling you to choose the books that are exactly right for your child:

Level 1 for Preschool to Grade 1
Level 2 for Grades 1 to 3
Level 3 for Grades 2 and 3
Level 4 for Grades 2 to 4

The "normal" age at which a child begins to read can be anywhere from three to eight years old, so these levels are intended only as a general guideline.

No matter which level you select, you can be sure that you are helping your child learn to read, then read to learn!

A DORLING KINDERSLEY BOOK
www.dk.com

Editor Rachel Harrison
Art Editor Jane Horne

Senior Editor Linda Esposito
Senior Art Editor
Diane Thistlethwaite
US Editor Regina Kahney
Production Melanie Dowland
Picture Researcher Frances Vargo
Jacket Designer Victoria Harvey

Natural History Consultant
Theresa Greenaway
Reading Consultant
Dr. Linda B. Gambrell Ph.D.

First American Edition, 2000
2 4 6 8 10 9 7 5 3 1
Published in the United States by Dorling Kindersley Publishing, Inc.
95 Madison Avenue, New York, New York 10016

Published in Great Britain by Dorling Kindersley Limited.

Wallace, Karen.
    Born to be a butterfly: / by Karen Wallace. – 1st American ed.
    p.cm. – (Dorling Kindersley readers)
    Summary: Simple text and photographs describes the stages by
which a butterfly develops from an egg.
    ISBN 0-7894-5705-9 (pbk) ISBN 0-7894-5704-0 (hc)
    1. Butterflies–Life cycles–Juvenile literature. [1. Butterflies–Life cycles.]
I. Title. II Series.

QL544.2.W35 2000
595.78'9–dc21
                                        99-086950

Color reproduction by Colourscan, Singapore
Printed and bound in China by L. Rex Printing Co. Ltd.

The publisher would like to thank the following for
their kind permission to reproduce their photographs:
Key: a=above, c=center, b=below, l=left, r=right, t=top

Aquila: Michael Edwards 4 inset, Anthony Cooper 29t; **Bruce Coleman
Collection:** 4–5, 7b, 8, 9, 10t, 12–13, 16–17, 18–19, Andrew Purcell
14–15, Jane Burton 20, Kim Taylor 22–23; **Dorling Kindersley:** Colin
Keates 5 inset; **Natural History Photographic Agency:** E.A. Janes 11,
Stephen Dalton 21r; **Oxford Scientific Films:** J.S. & E.J. Woolmer 10b;
Premaphotos Wildlife: 25, Ken Preston-Mafham 29c; **Richard Revels:**
7t, 28–29; **RSPCA Photolibrary:** Jonathan Plant 6, E.A. Janes 30–31;
Windrush Photos: Dennis Green 24, Frank Blackburn 26–27

DORLING KINDERSLEY READERS

BEGINNING
1
TO READ

Born to Be a
Butterfly

Written by Karen Wallace

DORLING KINDERSLEY PUBLISHING, INC.
www.dk.com

A butterfly flits
from flower to flower.
Her red-striped wings
shine in the sun.

wings

She touches the petals
with her feet and her feelers.

feelers

She looks for a leaf
where she can lay
her eggs.

A butterfly flits
from leaf to leaf.

On each little leaf
she lays one or two eggs.
She squeezes the eggs
out of her body.
The outside of each egg
is covered with a shell.

shell

A caterpillar grows
Inside each egg.
Soon one is ready
to hatch.

caterpillar

She bites through the shell
with her strong, sharp jaws.
She munches the leaves
around her.

The caterpillar makes
a tent from a leaf.

She hides from the birds,
who are sharp-eyed and hungry.

Hundreds of caterpillars
hatch alongside her.
Some are unlucky.
Hungry birds peck them.
Furry bats snatch them.
Spiders catch them.

The caterpillar is hungry.
She needs to grow
so she crawls from her leaf tent.
She climbs up strong stems
and clings to young leaves.

The caterpillar munches
and crunches
all the leaves she can find.

Munch!
Crunch!

The caterpillar munches
and crunches.
She gets bigger and bigger.
Her black and yellow skin
gets tighter and tighter.

skin

Suddenly the skin
starts to split open!
The caterpillar wriggles out
with a brand-new skin.

The caterpillar grows quickly.
She sheds her skin
four times
before she is fully grown.

She looks for
a leaf
that is sturdy
and strong.

She hangs upside down.

The caterpillar
is changing
into a chrysalis
(KRIS-uh-liss).

chrysalis

Outside,
her skin turns hard
to keep her safe.

Inside,
something amazing
is happening.

Then one day
the chrysalis splits open.
Something crawls out
into the sunshine.

legs

It has a head and six legs.
It has wings and a body.
What can it be?

A brand-new butterfly
rests in the sunshine!
She is too wet to fly.

She holds out her wings
to help them dry faster.

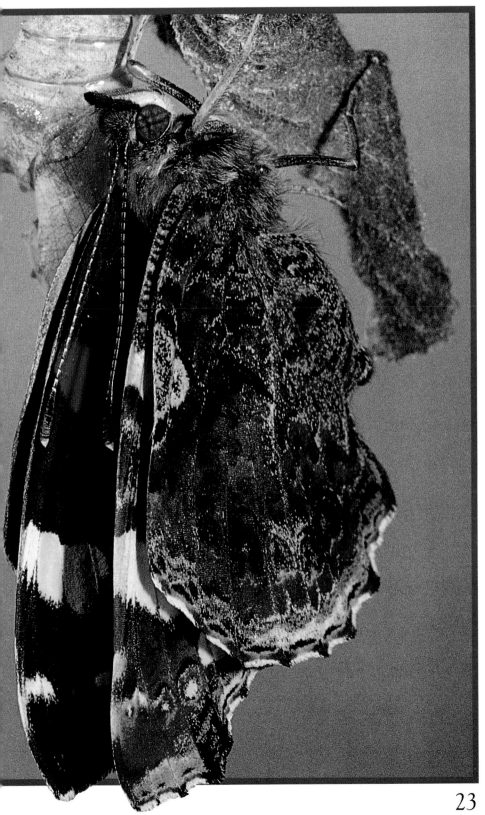

The butterfly flits
from flower to flower.
She sucks up the sweet nectar
with her long, hollow tongue.
When she is not eating,
her tongue is curled
like a spring.

tongue

Sometimes she rests
with her wings held together.
She looks brown as the tree bark
so hungry birds can't see her.

Now it is time
to look for a mate.
She finds him
sitting on a leaf.

They dance
in the sunshine
and fly off together.

The butterfly flits
from flower to flower.
Her red-striped wings
shine in the sun.

She looks for a leaf
where she can lay her eggs.

Soon, a hundred
more butterflies
will fly in the sun.

Picture Word List

wings
page 4

skin
page 15

feelers
page 5

chrysalis
page 18

shell
page 7

legs
page 21

caterpillar
page 8

tongue
page 25

32